WHAT IS BOWLING?

Written and Illustrated by
ANTHONY RAVIELLI

Atheneum/SMI, New York, 1975

Library of Congress Cataloging in Publication Data

Ravielli, Anthony.
What is bowling?

SUMMARY: Traces the history of bowling and explains
its "whats," "whys," and "hows" for young players.
1. Bowling—Juvenile literature. [1. Bowling]
I. Title.
GV903.5.R38   794.6   75-13572
ISBN 0-689-30492-7

Published simultaneously in Canada by McClelland & Stewart, Ltd.
Manufactured in the United States of America
First Edition

To George and Hazel

Bowling is one of the most popular games in the world. It is enjoyed by more than 30 million men, women and children in the United States alone.

But did you know that bowling is also one of the oldest games in the world? That it has been one of man's favorite pastimes since prehistoric days?

This is the story of bowling—how it began, how it evolved, and how it is played.

The act of bowling, or rolling an object at a standing target, goes back to the Stone Age, when cavemen set up rows of pointed rocks and tried to knock them over with heavy boulders.

In those prehistoric days, when man was learning to survive, bowling wasn't a game—more likely, it was a form of target practice. Cavemen probably bowled to sharpen their aim for hunting.

No one really knows who first got the idea to make bowling a sport. But we do know that, as long as 7,000 years ago, children in ancient Egypt played a game somewhat similar to modern tenpins. Stone artifacts resembling bowling-pins and balls were found among the playthings buried with the mummified remains of an Egyptian youth who, according to archaeologists, died in 5,200 B.C.

A crude version of bowling, called Ula Maika, was played by early Polynesians in the South Sea Islands. The object of Ula Maika was to hit oval-shaped pins with round stone discs rolled from 60 feet away. By a strange coincidence, this is the exact length of today's bowling lanes.

Throughout history, many games were invented and played that related to bowling in some way. One in particular, played outdoors without pins, originated in Egypt and made its way to Imperial Rome in 50 B.C.—more than 2,000 years ago.

In the Roman game, which they called Boccie, a small ball, or peg, served as a target. Players rolled a large ball toward the target and whoever came closest scored a point. To add more excitement, money was wagered on the outcome of each game.

Understandably, Boccie became the favorite pastime of Caesar's troops. It was played in army camps all over the Roman Empire, and remains to this day immensely popular among Italians.

Wherever the Roman Legions went, the game of Boccie went with them. They introduced it first to Northern Europe and later to England, where it evolved into the game of Bowles or Lawn Bowling.

Lawn Bowling got off to a flying start in 12th-century England. Its popularity spread over the entire Island and in time became the favorite form of gambling for rich and poor alike. In fact, Lawn Bowling was so widely played during the early 14th century that King Edward III banned the game because it interfered with the practice of archery—the military arms of the period.

Although these restrictions were never lifted, Lawn Bowling continued to flourish. The English people found ways to avoid detection and went right on bowling at fever pitch. Even Henry VIII, who himself issued edicts forbidding the game, played it privately in the grounds of his palaces.

Today, Lawn Bowling is still a leading outdoor sport in England and—along with golf—the national warm-weather sport of Scotland.

Indoor bowling, or bowling at pins, took its first step in Germany more than 1,600 years ago. It began in the monasteries of 300 A.D. and grew out of the superstitions of the time.

It was the custom for the peasants of that period to carry big, bottle-shaped clubs at all times—even to church. They called this weapon a "kegel," which is the German word for club.

At Sunday services, the presiding monks invented a ceremony to encourage churchgoing and to combat evil. They told the peasants that the kegel they carried represented the devil. To prove their devotion, the men were to stand the kegel up at the far end of a long, narrow hallway and to try to knock the devil down with a round rock rolled from the opposite end of the hallway. If they succeeded, they were absolved of sin. If, on the other hand, they missed, they would have to mend their ways and repent.

The monks were so fascinated by this excercise that eventually they began to try it themselves. To make a game of it, they increased the number of kegels.

To this day, modern bowling is sometimes referred to as kegling, and bowlers as keglers.

By 500 A.D. the rolling of stones at kegels had lost its religious meaning and had moved out of the monasteries into the homes of the wealthy.

Only the rich had the room and could afford to build bowling alleys. So, for a while, knocking kegels down remained the game of the nobility and the well-to-do.

As time went by, bowling at kegels found its way into army barracks, schools, and meeting rooms. Once it reached the people, the game quickly spread throughout Germany. By the Middle Ages, the game was played by peasant and noble alike on holidays and festive occasions.

But each section of the country had its own way of playing: Alleys varied in length; balls were of different sizes and weight; some districts played with three kegels, others with as many as 15.

During the 16th century, a movement to make the game uniform was encouraged by bowling enthusiasts, including Martin Luther, the famous religious leader. Nine kegels arranged in a diamond formation was agreed upon, and the game became officially Kegelspiel, or Ninepins.

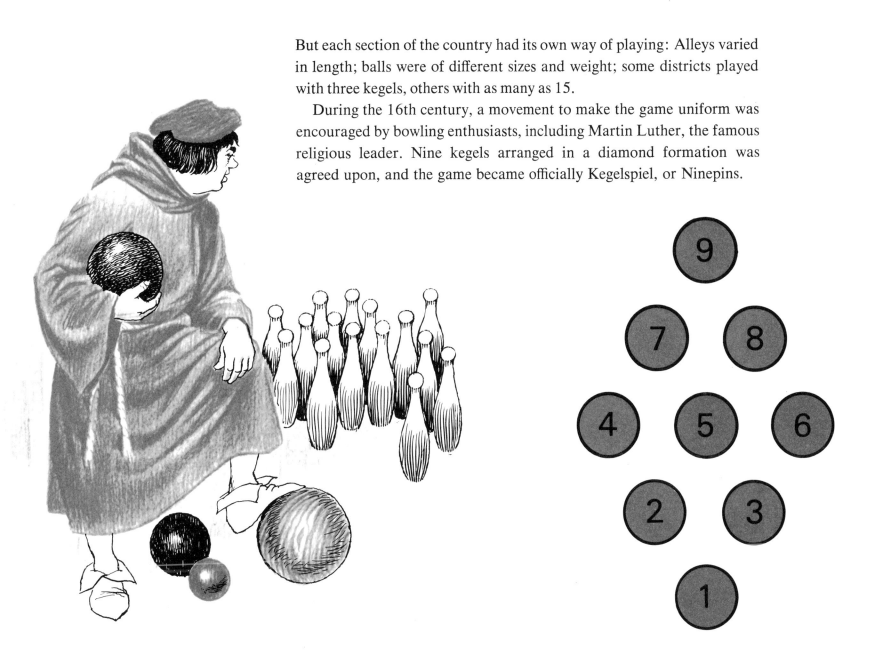

The game of ninepins spread from Germany to Holland and was brought from Holland to America by the early Dutch settlers of New Amsterdam, now the city of New York.

The Dutch preferred to bowl out-of-doors on a clay alley with a board laid flat upon the clay. The ball was rolled toward the pins on this narrow board.

There is no doubt that bowling was a popular sport among the early Dutch settlers of New Amsterdam. An area of a park at the lower end of Manhattan was set aside for the game. The settlers named it Bowling Green and it still bears that name to this day.

Ninepins was exported by the Dutch throughout New England. In New York State it worked its way up the Hudson River to the Catskills. When the superstitious settlers of the period heard summer thunder, they thought it was the sound of ninepins being played in the Catskill Mountains by the ghosts of Henry Hudson and his crew.

This superstition appears in the tale of Rip Van Winkle, except that the thunder was produced by those strange little men who spent all their time bowling at ninepins.

In the early 1800s, ninepins became extremely popular throughout the New England States. It reached a peak in New York, Connecticut and Massachusetts, where it was played mostly indoors.

Bowling places appeared everywhere in the heavily-populated areas of cities. In lower New York City, for example, there were lanes on nearly every block. Many of the bowling lanes were located in the basements and back rooms of saloons. The players were mostly patrons of these places, and as they generally liked to gamble it was not long before ninepins became more of a gambling game than a sport.

In those days, there was no standard equipment, lanes were bumpy and uneven, and, of course, there were no formal rules or regulations. Betting was heavy, games were rigged, and players were often cheated. Complaints reached the ears of lawmakers and the game of ninepins was outlawed.

The respectable people who enjoyed bowling as a sport found ways to get around the law which forbade the game of ninepins. They simply added an extra pin, changed the formation from a diamond to the familiar triangle we use today, and—presto! —the game of TENPINS was born!

Modern bowling, or tenpins, owes its success to the American Bowling Congress, which was formed in 1895 to govern the sport. The ABC not only supervised and promoted the game, they also established a set of rules, regulations and standards that are observed to this day wherever tenpins is played.

All bowling equipment is made to meet rigid ABC standards so that players everywhere compete under equal conditions.

The lane on which tenpins is played, for example, can be no more than 42 inches wide and 63 feet long. It must be smooth and highly polished with an approach area at its near end and, at its far end, a pit where fallen pins are discarded. A foul line separates the approach area from the lane.

Misthrown balls that roll off the lane are guided to the pit by way of nine-inch-wide gutters which run the length of the lane on either side.

It is on the furthermost section of the lane—called the pin deck— that the pins are placed, in a triangular formation. Each side of the triangle measures 36 inches, and the distance from the center of the head pin to the foul line is exactly 60 feet.

Pins conform to specific measurements and weights. They are bottle-shaped, 15 inches high, made of very hard maple, and covered with a plastic coating.

In the past, bowling balls were made of stone, wood or iron. Today's bowling balls are manufactured of either hard rubber or plastic. They cannot measure more than 27 inches in circumference nor weigh more than 16 pounds. Smaller balls, some weighing as little as eight pounds, are permissible and are frequently used by younger players.

To play the game well, special shoes are recommended with a rubber sole on one shoe and a leather sole on the other. We will see later why this is necessary.

The markers imbedded in the approach area, and the rangefinders imbedded in the lane beyond the foul line, are there to assist the bowler. Markers help the player to find the spot to stand on as he prepares to bowl and the path to take to the foul line. Rangefinders are for aiming and are usually the "targets" the bowler shoots for as he rolls the ball to the pins.

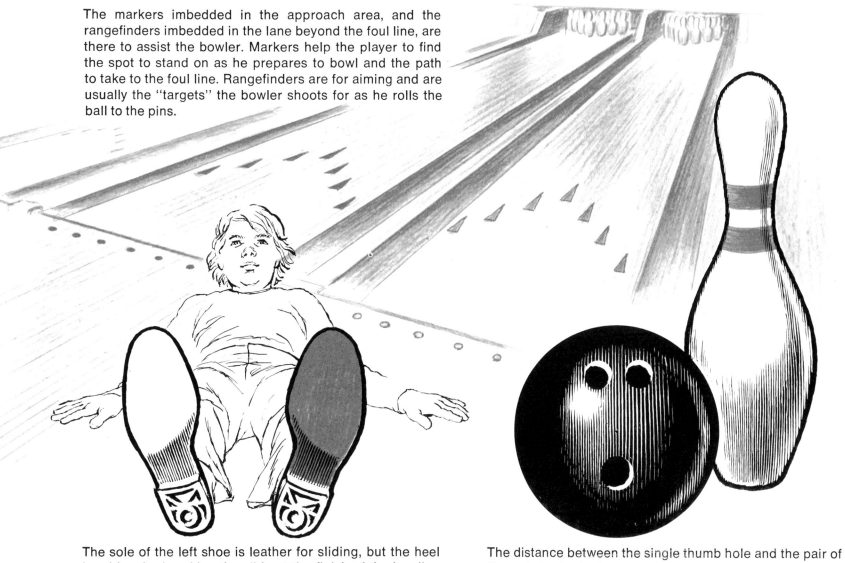

The sole of the left shoe is leather for sliding, but the heel is rubber for breaking the slide at the finish of the bowling action. (For left-handed players, the leather is on the right sole.)

The distance between the single thumb hole and the pair of finger holes in the bowling ball varies according to the size of the hand. (Left or right-handed players can use the same ball.)

Bowling is a simple game in that almost anyone can play. The difference between the good player and the not-so-good player is largely accuracy. And accuracy can be achieved with practice.

The first thing to do, if you want to become an accurate bowler, is to choose a suitable ball. This means one that is neither too heavy nor too light, but just comfortable for you. Then check the finger holes. Be sure to insert your thumb in the thumb hole as far as it will go, and check that it fits snugly but not tightly. Now let your fingers rest naturally on the ball. If the middle joints of your second and third fingers rest on the front edge of the finger holes, the ball is correct for you.

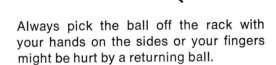

Always pick the ball off the rack with your hands on the sides or your fingers might be hurt by a returning ball.

THE PROPER GRIP—With your thumb fully inserted, place your second and third fingers in the holes and grip the ball firmly between the first and second joints of these fingers.

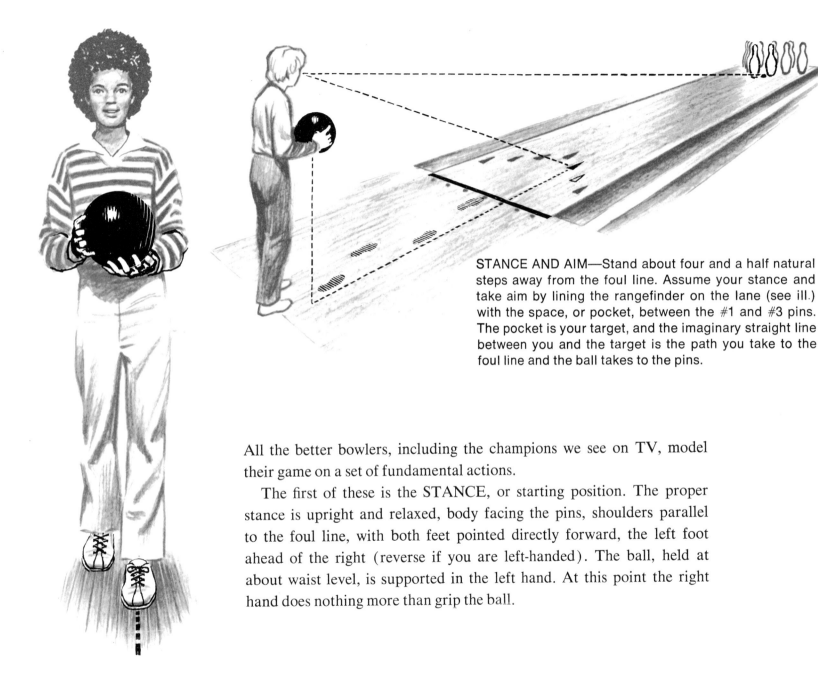

STANCE AND AIM—Stand about four and a half natural steps away from the foul line. Assume your stance and take aim by lining the rangefinder on the lane (see ill.) with the space, or pocket, between the #1 and #3 pins. The pocket is your target, and the imaginary straight line between you and the target is the path you take to the foul line and the ball takes to the pins.

All the better bowlers, including the champions we see on TV, model their game on a set of fundamental actions.

The first of these is the STANCE, or starting position. The proper stance is upright and relaxed, body facing the pins, shoulders parallel to the foul line, with both feet pointed directly forward, the left foot ahead of the right (reverse if you are left-handed). The ball, held at about waist level, is supported in the left hand. At this point the right hand does nothing more than grip the ball.

At the start of the delivery, move ball to right but keep elbow close to side.

Fig. 1. *Fig. 2.* *Fig. 3.*

The DELIVERY, or the action which carries you and the ball to within inches of the foul line, is made in four steps.

Fig. 1. Before you set the delivery in motion, shift the ball from the stance position to your right and lean slightly forward. Be sure your right elbow is close to your side. The ball, still supported by the left hand, is now on the target line and the right arm is in a position to swing freely from the shoulder in a pendulum motion.

Fig. 2. With your weight on your left side, take THE FIRST STEP with your right foot and at the same time push the ball *away* from you, letting the left hand help keep the ball on line.

Fig. 4.

Fig. 5.

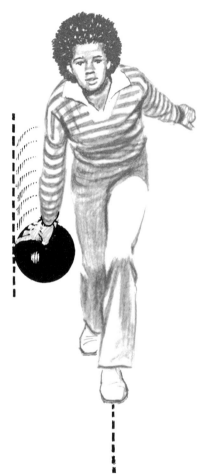

Fig. 3. During THE SECOND STEP, as your left hand leaves the ball and swings out to balance the body, your right arm lowers, straightens, and starts to move the ball backwards.

Fig. 4. At the end of THE THIRD STEP, your upper body is leaning forward and your right arm has carried the ball to the top of its backswing, which should never be higher than the shoulder.

Fig. 5. THE FOURTH STEP is mostly a slide. With the weight pressing down on your right foot, your left foot slides on its leather sole toward the foul line. Your right arm sweeps downward at the start of the fourth step and swings the ball forward, catching up with your sliding left foot.

Throughout delivery, ball and feet move on straight and parallel paths, shoulders square to foul line and eyes fixed on target.

The SLIDE, or fourth step, comes to an end about four inches before the foul line. At that point the rubber heel comes down to stop your left foot as your hand continues to move forward, carrying the ball over the line and releasing it.

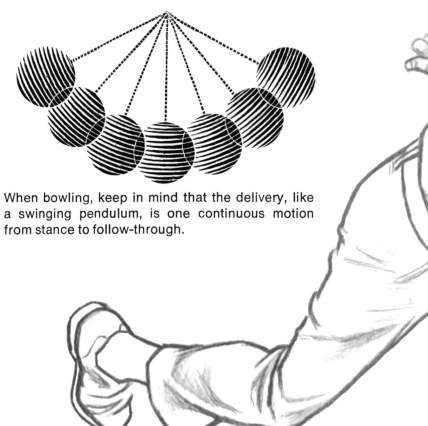

When bowling, keep in mind that the delivery, like a swinging pendulum, is one continuous motion from stance to follow-through.

The RELEASE (when the ball leaves the hand) is the climax of the delivery, and it must be a smooth, continuous action. Your thumb comes out first, followed almost immediately by your fingers as they give the ball a slight lift. Your hand and arm FOLLOW-THROUGH and continue to move straight ahead toward the target, as though "reaching for the pins." Your right arm, no longer pulled straight by the weight of the ball, may bend at the elbow as it completes the arc and continues up to the level of your head, or higher.

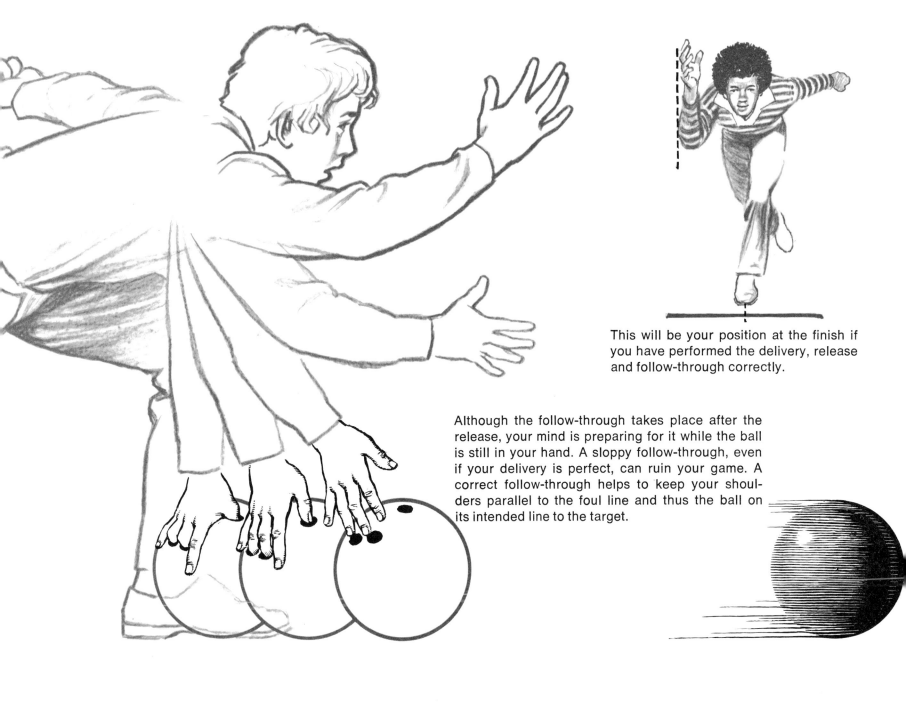

This will be your position at the finish if you have performed the delivery, release and follow-through correctly.

Although the follow-through takes place after the release, your mind is preparing for it while the ball is still in your hand. A sloppy follow-through, even if your delivery is perfect, can ruin your game. A correct follow-through helps to keep your shoulders parallel to the foul line and thus the ball on its intended line to the target.

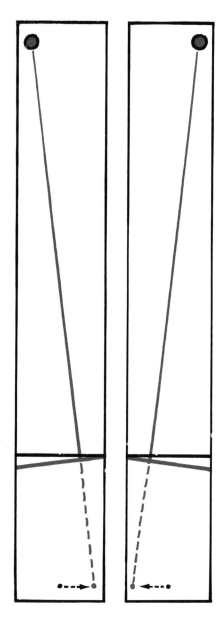

Picture an imaginary foul line at right angles to the target.

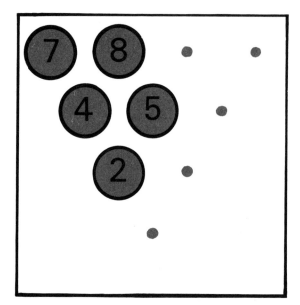

Spares made by moving to the right of center

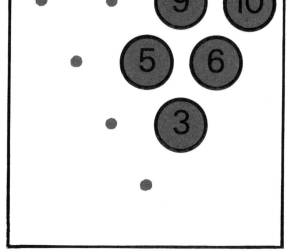

Spares made by moving to the left of center

THE SECOND BALL

A game of bowling is divided into 10 frames. Two balls are rolled in each frame. The ideal is to score a STRIKE by toppling all 10 pins with the first roll. But that doesn't always happen. The next best thing is to make a SPARE, by toppling all pins left standing after the first roll with the second roll of the ball.

In shooting for spares, the delivery, release and follow-through are the same as outlined in the previous pages. Only your position changes because your target may have moved to the right or the left side of the lane, depending on where the pins are left standing.

STRIKE

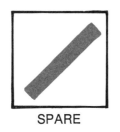
SPARE

MISS

SPLIT

SPLIT SPARED

SCORING

A bowling scoresheet consists of 10 boxes, each box representing a frame. You roll two balls to complete a frame unless you score a strike, in which case the one ball constitutes the frame. A strike earns the bowler 10 points, plus the total of pins knocked down on his next *two* rolls. A spare is also 10 points plus the number of pins knocked down on just the *next* roll. Making less than 10 pins with two rolls of the ball is called a MISS or an ERROR, which gives the bowler a point for every pin knocked down in a frame and nothing more. A SPLIT occurs when two or more pins are left standing after the first roll and are so wide apart that a ball can roll between the pins and leave them untouched. Splits are not scored as misses. They are rarely converted into spares, but sometimes a bowler gets lucky and "spares out"—knocks down the remaining pins.

1	2	3	4	5	6	7	8	9	10	TOTAL
−	/	−	o	X	/	−	∅	/	X X 7	
9	24	31	40	60	77	85	102	122	149	149

This is a sample scoresheet. The small squares in the upper right-hand corner of the boxes are to mark the symbols representing strikes, spares, misses, or splits. The large boxes are to mark the number of pins you knock down plus your rewards, adding each new amount to the previous one.

DO'S AND DON'TS

- Always carry the ball with both hands until you are into your delivery. Otherwise your bowling hand will tire before the game is finished.

- When you take your stance, be sure your feet are pointed at the target and that your shoulders are parallel with the foul line. Remember, the ball travels in the direction you are facing.

- Don't turn your shoulders at the top of the backswing. Twisting brings the ball behind your body, which means that you will have to swing it *around* your body on the downswing and thus across the lane into the gutter on release.

- The same thing will happen if you swing your arm *away* from your body on the backswing. "Sidewheeling" and "sidearming" can be prevented by keeping your elbow close to your body at the start of the delivery and your shoulders square to the pins throughout the swing. Keep in mind that a pendulum swings back and forth on a straight line.

- Above all, do not rush your delivery. Neither speed nor great power can substitute for accuracy in rolling a good score.

- And finally, DON'T RELEASE THE BALL IN AN UPRIGHT POSITION! "Lofting" can damage the ball, the lane and your score. Be certain that at release your left knee is bent, your body is leaning forward, and your ball is no more than an inch or two above the floor of the lane.

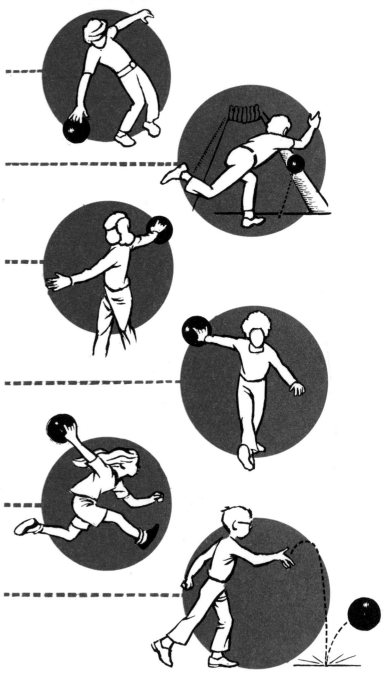

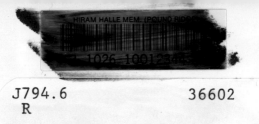
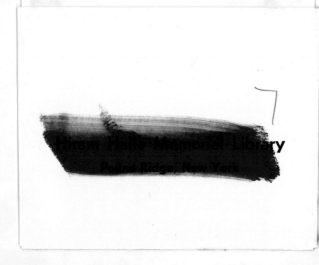